Robert Desnos

Night of Loveless Nights

translated from French by Lewis Warsh
with an afterword by David Rosenberg

Winter Editions, 2023

Artwork by David Rosenberg
for the cover of *Night of Loveless Nights*
(*The Ant's Forefoot* #10, New York, 1973)

Night of Loveless Nights

Nuit putride et glaciale, épouvantable nuit,
Nuit du fantôme infirme et des plantes pourries,
Incandescente nuit, flamme et feu dans les puits,
Ténèbres sans éclairs, mensonges et rouable.

Qui me regarde ainsi au fracas des rivières?
Noyés, pêcheurs, marins? Éclatez les tumeurs
Malignes sur la peau des ombres passagères,
Ces yeux m'ont déjà vu, retentissez clameurs!

Le soleil ce jour-là couchait dans la cité
L'ombre des marronniers au pied des édifices,
Les étendards claquaient sur les tours et l'été
Amoncelait ses fruits pour d'annuels sacrifices.

Tu viens de loin, c'est entendu, vomisseur de couleuvres,
Héros, bien sûr, assassin morne, l'amoureux
Sans douleur disparaît, et toi, fils de tes œuvres
Suicidé, rougis-tu du désir d'être heureux?

Fantôme, c'est ma glace où la nuit se prolonge
Parmi les cercueils froids et les cœurs dégoutants,
L'amour cuit et recuit comme une fausse oronge
Et l'ombre d'une amante aux mains d'un impotent.

Et pourtant tu n'es pas de ceux que je dédaigne.
Ah! serrons-nous les mains, mon frère, embrassons-nous
Parmi les billets doux, les rubans et les peignes,
La prière jamais n'a sali tes genoux.

Hideous night, putrid and glacial,
Night of disabled ghosts and rotting plants,
Incandescent night, flame and fire in the pits,
Shades of darkness without lightning, duplicity and lies.

Who sees rivers crashing inside himself?
Suicides, trespassers, sailors? Explode
Malignant tumors on the skin of passing shadows,
These eyes have already seen me, shouts resound!

Earlier today the sun was setting in the city
Shadows of chestnut trees at the foot of buildings,
Banners snapped in the wind on the towers and summer
Heaped its fruits for the annual sacrifices.

You come at a distance, that's for sure, vomiting snakes,
Hero, of course, gloomy assassin, lover
Whose pain never dies, and you, son of your works,
Suicide, do you blush with the desire to be happy?

Ghost, it is my mirror where night continues
Among the cold coffins and the bleeding hearts,
Love cooked and recooked like orange acid
The shadow of a lover in a cripple's hands.

And still you are not one of those I scorn.
Ah! let us shake hands, my brother, let us embrace
Among the love letters, ribbons and combs,
You never soiled your knees praying.

Tu cherchais dans la plage aux pieds des rochers droits
La crique où vont s'échouer les étoiles marines :
C'était le soir, des feux à travers le ciel froid
Naviguaient et, rêvant au milieu des salines,

Tu voyais circuler des frégates sans nom
Dans l'éclaboussement des chutes impossibles.
Où sont ces soirs? Ô flots rechargez vos canons
Car le ciel en rumeur est encombré de cibles.

Quel destin t'enchaîna pour servir les sévères,
Celles dont les cheveux charment les colibris,
Celles dont les seins durs sont un fatal abri
Et celles dont la nuque est un nid de mystère,

Celles rencontrées nues dans les nuits de naufrage,
Celles des incendies et celles des déserts,
Celles qui sont flétries par l'amour avant l'âge,
Celles qui pour mentir gardent les yeux sincères,

Celles au cœur profond, celles aux belles jambes,
Celles dont le sourire est subtil et méchant,
Celles dont la tendresse est un diamant qui flambe
Et celles dont les reins balancent en marchant,

Celles dont la culotte étroite étreint les cuisses,
Celles qui, sous la jupe, ont un pantalon blanc
Laissant un peu de chair libre par artifice
Entre la jarretière et le flots des volants,

You were searching the shore at the foot of the vertical rocks
At the creek where the navies of stars wash up:
It was evening, some lightning bolts were sailing through
The cold sky and dreaming in the middle of the salt marsh

You saw nameless frigates moving
In the splashing of impossible drops.
Where are these evenings? O waves recharge your cannons
For the roaring sky is crowded with targets.

What destiny linked you to serve the most severe,
Those whose hair charmed the humming birds,
Whose hard breasts are a fatal refuge
And to whom the nape of the neck is a nest of mystery,

Those high clouds encountered in the shipwrecked nights,
Those of fires and those of deserts,
Those withered by love before their time,
Those who lie to protect their openness,

Those with heavy hearts, those with beautiful legs,
Those whose smiles are subtle and wicked,
Those to whom tenderness is a blazing diamond
And those whose muscles ripple while walking,

Those whose tight trousers hug their thighs,
Who, under their skirts, wear a pair of white pants
Leaving a little bare flesh to beguile
Between the garter and the waves of the rising dresses,

Celles que tu suivis dans l'espoir ou le doute,
Celles que tu suivis ne se retournaient pas
Et les bouquets fanés qu'elles jetaient en route
T'entraînèrent longtemps au hasard de leurs pas

Mais tu les poursuivras à la mort sans répit,
Les yeux las de percer des ténèbres moroses,
De voir lever le jour sur le ciel de leur lit
Et d'abriter leur ombre en tes prunelles closes.

Une rose à la bouche et les yeux caressants
Elles s'acharneront avec des mains cruelles
À torturer ton cœur, à répandre ton sang
Comme pour les punir d'avoir battu pour elles.

Heureux s'il suffisait, pour se faire aimer d'elles,
D'affronter sans faiblir des dangers merveilleux
Et de toujours garder l'âme et le cœur fidèle
Pour lire la tendresse aux éclairs de leurs yeux,

Mais les plus audacieux, sinon les plus sincères,
Volent à pleine bouche à leur bouche un aveu
Et devant nos pensées, comme aux proues les chimères,
Resplendit leur sourire et flottent leurs cheveux.

Car l'unique régit l'amour et ses douleurs,
Lui seul a possédé les âmes passionnées
Les uns s'étant soumis à sa loi par malheur
N'ont connu qu'un bourreau pendant maintes années.

Those whom you followed in hope or in doubt
Those whom you followed were not returning
And the faded bouquets they dropped on the way
Induced you to follow them randomly for awhile.

But you would pursue them to death without delay,
Tired eyes piercing gloomy shades of gray,
To see day breaking in the sky above their bed
And shelter their shadows in your closed pupils.

A rose opens and caresses your eyes
She will work with cruel hands
To torture your heart, to spill your blood
As if she were punishing herself by hurting you.

Happy if he were good enough to love them,
To confront unyielding the marvelous risks
And always keep the spirit and heart faithful
In order to read the gentle lights of their eyes.

But the boldest, unless they're incredibly sincere,
Steal—and moments later they're confessing,
And before our thoughts, like the prows of our dreams,
Their smiles gleam and their hair is floating.

Only the unique man rules love and its sorrows,
Only him possessing a passionate spirit
The ones who submitted to the laws of unhappiness
Have known only a hangman for many years.

D'autres l'ont poursuivi dans ses métamorphoses :
Après les yeux très bleus voici les yeux très noir
Brillant dans un visage où se flétrit la rose,
Plus profonds que le ciel et que le désespoir.

Maître de leur sommeil et de leurs insomnies
Il les entraîne en foule, à travers les pays,
Vers des mers éventrées et des épiphanies...
La marée sera haute et l'étoile a failli.

Quelqu'un m'a raconté que, perdu dans les glaces,
Dans un chaos de monts, loin de tout océan,
Il vit passer, sans heurt et sans fumée, la masse
Immense et pavoisée d'un paquebot géant.

Des marins silencieux s'accrochaient aux cordages
Et des oiseaux gueulards volaient dans les haubans
Des danseuses rêvaient au bord des bastingages
En robes de soirée et coiffées de turbans.

Les bijoux entouraient d'étincelles glaciales
Leur gorge et leurs poignets et de grands éventails
De plumes, dans leurs mains, claquaient vers des escales
Où les bals rougissaient les tours et les portails.

Les danseurs abîmés dans leur mélancolie
En songe comparaient leurs désirs à l'acier.
C'était parmi les monts, dans un soir de folie,
De grands nuages coulaient sur le flanc des glaciers.

Others continued to go through changes:
After the very blue eyes here are the very black eyes
Brightening a face where the color has faded
Vaster than the sky, and the vast face of despair.

Master of their sleep and sleeplessness
He carried them in the crowd, across the land,
Towards the open seas and the epiphanies. .
The tide will be high and the stars falling.

Someone once told me that, lost in the ice,
On a range of mountains far from the ocean,
He passed, without colliding or blowing smoke,
The immense mass of a giant steamship decked with flags.

Silent sailors hung from ropes
And noisy birds blew in the shrouds
Some dancers were dreaming at the end of the railings
Wearing turbans and evening gowns.

Jewels of icy sparks surrounded
Their throats and wrists and great fans
Of feathers, in their hands, snapped to attention
Balls of fire reddening the towers and portals.

The dancers engulfed in their sadness
In a dream compared their desires to steel.
It was among the mountains, on an evening of madness,
As great clouds floated over the icy slopes.

Un autre découvrit, au creux d'une clairière,
Un rosier florissant entouré de sapins.
Combien a-t-il cueilli de roses sanguinaires
Avant de s'endormir sous la mousse au matin?

Mais ses yeux ont gardé l'étrange paysage
Inscrit sur leur prunelle et son cœur incertain
A choisi pour cesser de battre sans courage
Ce lieu clos par l'odeur de la rose et du thym.

Du temps où nous chantions avec des voix vibrantes
Nous avons traversé ces pays singuliers
Où l'écho répondait aux questions des amantes
Par des mots dont le sens nous était familier.

Mais, depuis que la nuit s'écroule sur nos têtes,
Ces mots ont dans nos cœurs des accents mystérieux
Et quand un souvenir parfois nous les répète
Nous désobéissons à leur ordre impérieux.

Entendez-vous chanter des voix dans les montagnes
Et retentir le bruit des cors et des buccins?
Pourquoi ne chantons-nous que les refrain du bagne
Au son d'un éternel et lugubre tocsin?

Serait-ce pas Don Juan qui parcourt ces allées
Où l'ombre se marie aux spectres de l'amour?
Ce pas qui retentit dans les nuits désolées
A-t-il marqué les cœurs avec un talon lourd?

Another discovered, deep in a clearing,
A flourishing rose tree surrounded by firs.
How many of the bloody roses did he pluck
Before falling asleep at dawn under the moss?

But these eyes have kept the strange landscape
Inscribed on their pupils and his uncertain heart
Has chosen to stop beating without courage
In this place closed by the odor of rose and thyme.

From a time when we sang with vibrant voices
We have crossed these strange countries
Where the echo answered the lovers' questions
With words whose sense was familiar to us.

But, since the night collapses on our heads,
These words have mysterious accents in our hearts
And when a memory sometimes recurs to us
We disobey its urgent order.

Do you know the singing of voices in the mountains
The resounding noise of trumpets and horns?
Why are we only singing the refrains of imprisonment
To the endless sound of a sad alarm?

Wasn't it Don Juan who ran down these alleys
Where a shadow married him to the ghosts of love?
Why has this step which resounds in the desolate night
Marked our hearts with its heavy tread?

Ce n'est pas le Don Juan qui descend impassible
L'escalier ruisselant d'infernales splendeurs
Ni celui qui crachait aux versets de la Bible
Et but en ricanant avec le commandeur.

Ses beaux yeux incompris n'ont pas touché les cœurs,
Sa bouche n'a connu que le baiser du rêve,
Et c'est celui que rêve en de sombres ardeurs
Celle qui le dédaigne et l'ignore et sans trêve

Heurte ses diamants froids, ses lèvres sépulcrales,
Sa bouche silencieuse à sa bouche et ses yeux,
Ses yeux de sphinx cruels et ses mains animales
A ses yeux, a ses mains, à son étoile, aux cieux.

Mais lui, le cœur meurtri par de mortes chimères,
Gardant leur bec pourri planté dans ses amours,
Pour un baiser viril, ô beautés éphémères,
Vous sauvera sans doute au seuil du dernier jour.

Le rire sur sa bouche écrasera des fraises
Ses yeux seront marqués par un plus pur destin.
C'est Bacchus renaissant des cendres et des braises,
Les cendres dans les dents, les braises dans les mains.

Mais pour un qui renaît combien qui, sans mourir,
Portent au cœur, portent aux pieds de lourdes chaînes.
Les fleuves couleront et les morts vont pourrir...
Chaque an reverdira le feuillage des chênes.

This isn't Don Juan who impassively descends
The staircase streaming with infernal splendors
Nor the one who spits forth verses from the Bible
Sneering while having a drink with god.

These beautiful misunderstood eyes have not touched
    the hearts,
This mouth has known only the kiss of dreams,
And it is the one who dreams in the warm gloom
One who despises and ignores him without truce

Lips like sepulchers, their cold diamonds collide,
Mouth at peace against mouth and eyes,
Eyes like a cruel sphinx and hands like an animal's,
To the eyes, the hands, the stars, the skies.

But for him, heart bruised by dead dreams,
He preserves the rotten beak planted in their love,
For a virile kiss, O fleeting beauties,
You will run without doubt to the threshold of the last day.

The laughter on her mouth will crush some strawberries,
Her eyes will be marked by a purer destiny.
It is Bacchus reviving the ashes and the glowing embers,
Ashes for the teeth, embers for the hands.

But for one who returned without dying,
They support the heart and the legs with heavy chains.
The rivers will flow and the dead will rot...
Each year the leaves of the oaks will turn green.

J'habite quand il me plaît un ravin ténébreux au-dessus duquel le ciel se découpe en un losange déchiqueté par l'ombre des sapins des mélèzes et des rochers qui couvrent les pentes escarpées.

Dans l'herbe du ravin poussent d'étranges tubéreuses des ancolies et des colchiques survolées par des libellules et des mantes religieuses et si pareils sans cesse le ciel la flore et la faune où succèdent aux insectes les corneilles moroses et les rats musqués que je ne sais quelle immuable saison s'est abattue sur ce toujours nocturne ravin avec son dais en losange constellé que ne traverse aucun nuage.

Sur les troncs des arbres deux initiales toujours les mêmes sont gravées. Par quel couteau par quelle main pour quel cœur ?

Le vallon était désert quand j'y vins pour la première fois. Nul n'y était venu avant moi. Nul autre que moi ne l'a parcouru.

La mare où les grenouilles nagent dans l'ombre avec des mouvements réguliers reflète des étoiles immobiles et le marais que les crapauds peuplent de leur cri sonore et triste possède un feu follet toujours le même.

La saison de l'amour triste et immobile plane en cette solitude.

Je l'aimerai toujours et sans doute ne pourrai-je jamais franchir l'orée des mélèzes et des sapins escalader les rochers baroques pour atteindre la route blanche où elle passe à certaines heures. La route où les ombres n'ont pas toujours la même direction.

Parfois il me semble que la nuit vient seulement de s'abattre. Des chasseurs passent sur la route que je ne vois pas. Le chant de cors de chasse résonne sous les mélèzes. La journée a été

I live when it pleases me in dark ravine below which the sky has cut out the shape of a jagged diamond from the shadows of the fir trees, the larches and the rocks which cover the steep slope.

In the grass of the ravine grow strange tubers, some columbine and colchicums around which dragonflies and praying mantis fly without stopping, the sky the flora and the fauna where the insects are followed by gloomy crows and muskrats, so that I do not know which immutable season has swooped down onto this always nocturnal ravine, with its canopy of a diamond constellation which no cloud has ever passed.

On the tree trunks the same two initials are always carved. By what knife, what hand, what heart?

The small valley was deserted when I came there for the first time. No one had come there before me. No other but myself had traveled there.

The pond where the frogs swim in the shadow with steady movements reflects the immobile stars and the marsh where the toads live and the sad and sombre cry of the will-o-wisp always the same.

The season of love, sad and still, hangs over this solitude.

I will love it always and without doubt I will never be able to go beyond the border of larches and fir trees, to scale the baroque rocks, in order to reach the white road where she passes at certain hours. The road where the shadows do not always fall in the same direction.

Sometimes it seems to me that the night comes to fall on me alone. Hunters pass on the road which I cannot see. The song of the hunting horns resonates under the larches. The trip has been long, among the workers of the earth, in pursuit of

longue parmi les terres de labour à la poursuite du renard du blaireau et du chevreuil. Le naseau des chevaux fume blanc dans la nuit.

Les airs de chasse s'éteignent. Et je déchiffre difficilement les initiales identiques sur le tronc des mélèzes qui bornent le ravin.

Nulle étoile en tombant n'a fait jaillir l'écume,
Rien ne trouble les monts, les cieux, le feu, les eaux,
Excepté cet envol horizontal de plumes
Qui révèle la chute et la mort d'un oiseau.

Et rien n'arrêtera cette plume envolée,
Ni les cheveux luisants d'un cavalier sauvage,
Ni l'encre méprisable au fond d'un encrier,
Ni la vague chantante et le grondant orage,

Ni le cou séduisant des belles misérables,
Ni la branche de l'arbre et le tombeau fermé,
Ni les bateaux qui font la nuit grincer des câbles,
Ni le mur où des cœurs par des noms sont formés,

Ni le chant des lépreux dans les marais austères,
Ni la glace qui dort au fond des avenues
En reflétant sans cesse un tremblant réverbère
Et jamais, belle neige, un corps de femme nue,

Ni les monstres marins aux écailles fumeuses,
Ni les brouillards du nord avec leurs plaies d'azur,
Ni la vitre où le soir une femme rêveuse
Retrace en sa mémoire un amour au futur,

the fox, the badger or the deer. Nostrils of horses breathe white smoke in the night.

The air of the chase is extinguished. And I decipher with difficulty the identical initials on the trunk of the larch trees which border the ravine.

No shooting star bursts forth from the foam,
Nothing troubles the mountains, the skies, the fire, the waters,
Except for the horizontal flight of feathers
Which reveals the fall & the death of a bird.

And nothing will stop the flight of the feathers,
Neither the shining hair of a savage horseman,
Nor the contemptible ink at the bottom of an inkwell,
Nor the vague singsong of the rumbling storm,

Nor the seductive necks of the beautiful, miserable women,
Nor the branch of the tree and the closed tomb,
Nor the boats with creaking ropes which sail through the night,
Nor the wall where hearts are formed out of names.

Nor the song of the lepers in the desolate marsh,
Nor the ice which rests at the end of the streets
Reflecting without stop a trembling streetlight
And a woman's naked body in the beautiful snow,

Nor the sea monsters with smoky shells,
Nor the northern fogs with their azure sores,
Nor the windowpane where in the evening a woman muses
Tracing in her mind a future love,

Ni l'écho des appels d'un voyageur perdu,
Ni les nuages fuyards, ni les chevaux en marche,
Ni l'ombre d'un plongeur sur les quais et les arches,
Ni celle du pavé à son cou suspendu,

Ni toi Fouquier-Tinville aux mains de cire claire :
Les étoiles, les mains, l'amour, les yeux, le sang
Sont autant de fusées surgissant d'un cratère.
Adieu! C'est le matin blanchi comme un brisant.

Ô mains qui voudriez vous meurtrir à l'amour
Nous saurons vous donner le plus rouge baptême
Près duquel pâliront le feu des hauts fourneaux
Et le soleil mourant au sein des brouillards blêmes.

Les plus beaux yeux du monde ont connu nos pensées,
Nous avons essayé tous les vices fameux,
Mais les baisers et les luxures insensées
N'ont pas éteint l'espoir dans nos cœurs douloureux.

Je vis alors s'ouvrir des portes de cristal
Sur le cristal plus pur d'un fantôme adorable :
« Jetez dans le ruisseau votre cœur de métal
« Et brisez les flacons sur le marbre des tables!

« Crevez vos yeux et vos tympans et que vos langues
« Par vos bouches crachées soient mangées par les chiens,
« Dites adieu à vos désirs, bateaux qui tanguent,
« Que vos mains et vos pieds soient meurtris par des liens!

Nor the echo of the cries of a lost voyager,
Nor the fugitive clouds, nor the marching horses,
Nor the shadow of a diver from the quays and the arches,
Nor the pavement under his suspended neck,

Nor you Fouquier-Tinville with your hands of clear wax:
The stars, the hands, love, the eyes, the blood
Are like rockets rising from a crater.
Goodbye! This morning is white as surf.

O hands that would want to be bruised by love
We will know how to give you the bloodiest baptism
Already they are pale from the fire of the gas range
And the sun is dying on the breast of the dense fog.

The most beautiful eyes of the world have known our thoughts,
We have tried all the famous vices,
But the kisses and the senseless luxuries
Have not extinguished the hope in our unhappy hearts.

Then I saw the crystal doors fly open
On the purest crystal a divine phantom:
"Throw into the river your metal heart
And break these flagons on the marble tables!

Open your eyes and ears and with your tongue.
Spit from your mouth what may be eaten by the dogs
Say goodbye to your desires, let your boats sail away,
May your hands and feet be bruised by chains!

« Soyez humbles, perdez au courant de vos transes
« Votre espoir, votre orgueil et votre dignité
« Pour que je puisse encore augmenter vos souffrances
« En instituant sur vous d'exquises cruautés. »

C'est elle qui parla. C'est aussi l'amoureuse,
C'est le cœur de cristal et les yeux sans pitié,
Les plus beaux yeux du monde, ô sources lumineuses,
La belle bouche avec des dents de carnassier.

Enfonce tes deux mains dans mon cerveau docile,
Mords ma lèvre en feignant de m'offrir un baiser,
Si la force et l'orgueil sont des vertus faciles,
Dure est la solitude à l'amour imposée.

Je parlais d'un fantôme et d'un oiseau qui tombe,
Mon rêve perd les mots que ma bouche employait.
La prairie où je parle est creusée par les tombes
Et l'écho retentit du bruit clair des maillets.

On dresse l'échafaud dans la prison prochaine.
Le condamné qui dort dans un lit trop étroit
Rêve des grands corbeaux qui survolaient la plaine
Quand il y rencontra le désir et l'effroi.

Ces deux spectres zélés cheminaient côte à côte
Déchirant leur manteau et leur face aux branchages,
De faux amants frappés sans merci par leur faute
A leur suite faisaient un long pèlerinage.

Be humble, forget the waves of your fears,
Your hope, your pride and your dignity,
So that I will be able to increase your sufferings
And perform upon you some exquisite acts of cruelty."

It's she who speaks. It's my sweetheart.
It's the crystal heart and the eyes without pity,
The most beautiful eyes in the world, luminous sources,
The beautiful mouth with the meat-eating teeth.

I hold your hands against my docile brain,
Idly biting my lips while offering you a kiss,
If strength and pride are easy virtues
Hard is the solitude of self-imposed love.

I was speaking of a ghost and a falling bird,
My dream lost the words which my lips stammered,
The meadow where I speak is hallowed by graves
And the echo resounds of the distant noise of hammers.

One raises the gallows in the next prison.
The condemned man sleeping in a narrow bed
Dreams enormous ravens fly over the plain
When he encounters there desire and fear.

These two zealous ghosts walk side by side
Tearing their coats and faces on the branches,
While false lovers stricken unmercifully by their loss
Follow after them on a long pilgrimage.

Des incendies sifflaient sur les toits des hameaux.
Les poissons attirés par de célestes nasses
Montaient avec lenteur à travers les rameaux.
Des bûcherons sortaient de leurs chaumières basses.

Le condamné qui dort parlait avec l'un d'eux,
Plus spectral que le chêne où se plantait la hache :
« Écoutez, disait-il, mugir au loin les bœufs,
Le vent qui souffle ici brisera leur attache. »

Écoute jusqu'au jour la voix de la cruelle,
Sa bouche a la saveur d'un fruit empoisonné,
Le ciel et la montagne où les troupeaux s'appellent
Viennent de se confondre à nos yeux étonnés.

Charmé par les oiseaux, et par l'amour trompé,
Dans de noirs corridors, sous de sombres portiques,
L'amant recherchera la marque de l'épée
Qu'Isis au cœur de feu dans son cœur a trempée...
Ô lame au fil parfait, sœur des fleuves mystiques!

   L'oiseau qui chantait pour elle
   Dans sa cage ne chante plus
   Et la reine des hirondelles
   Ne tourne plus, ne tourne plus.

Un jour j'ai rencontré le vautour et l'orfraie.
Leur ombre sur le sol ne m'a pas étonné.
J'ai déchiffré plus tard sur des remparts de craie
L'initiale au charbon d'un nom que je connais.

Fires hiss on the roofs of the villages.
Fish drawn towards heavenly traps
Climb sluggishly through the branches.
Some woodcutters stand outside their cottages.

The condemned man who was sleeping spoke to one of them
More ghostly than the oak where the hatchet was planted:
"Listen," he said, "to the mooing of the far-off cows
The wind blowing here will break their chains."

Listen until daybreak when the voice of a cruel person,
His mouth has the taste of poisoned fruit,
Calls to the sky and the mountain where the herds
Are coming like blurs to our astonished eyes.

Charmed by the birds, and by frustrated love,
In black hallways, under sombre porticos,
The lover will look for the mark of the sword
Which Isis has dipped to the heart of the fire in her heart...
O wave of perfect thread, sister of mystic rivers!

> The bird who sang for her
> In her cage is no longer singing
> And the queen of the swallows
> No longer turns, no longer turns.

One day I met the vulture and the seahawk.
Their shadow on the sun did not astonish me.
Much later I made out on the chalk ramparts
The carbon initial of a name I knew.

Un vampire a frappé ma vitre de son aile :
Qu'il entre, couronné des algues de l'étang,
Avec son beau collier de vives coccinelles
Qui prédisent l'amour, la pluie et le beau temps.

Coucher avec elle
Pour le sommeil côte à côte
Pour les rêves parallèles
Pour la double respiration

Coucher avec elle
Pour l'ombre unique et surprenante
Pour la même chaleur
Pour la même solitude

Coucher avec elle
Pour l'aurore partagée
Pour le minuit identique
Pour les mêmes fantômes

Coucher coucher avec elle
Pour l'amour absolu
Pour le vice pour le vice
Pour les baisers de toute espèce

Coucher avec elle
Pour un naufrage ineffable
Pour se prostituer l'un à l'autre
Pour se confondre

A vampire struck my windowpane with its wing
Then he entered, crowned by the seaweed from the pond
With its collar of living ladybirds
Which foretold love, the rain and the beautiful days.

> *To sleep with her*
> *And lie side by side*
> *Dreaming the same dreams*
> *Our breaths mingling*
>
> *To sleep with her*
> *For the unique and amazing shadow*
> *For the same heat*
> *And the same solitude*
>
> *To sleep with her*
> *And share the same dawn*
> *The same moments*
> *The same ghosts*
>
> *To really sleep with her*
> *For the absolute love*
> *For the true vice*
> *And the embrace of all species*
>
> *To sleep with her*
> *For the ineffable shipwreck*
> *In order to prostitute each other*
> *To mingle all parts of ourselves totally*

Coucher avec elle
Pour se prouver et prouver vraiment
Que jamais n'a pesé sur l'âme et le corps des amants
Le mensonge d'une tache originelle

Toujours avoir le plus grand amour pour elle
N'est pas difficile
Mais tout est douteux pour les cœurs de feu, pour les
    cœurs fidèles

Toujours avoir le plus grand amour
Y a-t-il des trahisons involontaires
Non la chair n'est jamais menteuse
Et le corps du plus vicieux reste pur

Pur comme le plus grand amour pour elle
Dans mon seul cœur il fleurit sans contrainte
Nulle boue jamais n'atteignit l'image de celle
La seule aimée dans le cœur de l'amant.

Nulle boue jamais n'atteignit le plus grand amour pour elle
C'est pour sa pureté qu'on admire le diamant
Nulle boue ne tache le diamant ni le cœur de celle
La plus aimée dans le cœur de l'amant

Le plus sincère amant capable du plus grand amour
N'est pas un chaste ni un ascète ni un puritain
Et s'il éprouve le corps des plus belles
C'est qu'il sait bien que le plus beau est celui de l'aimée

To sleep with her
So as to prove and to prove truly
That never has there weighed on the souls and bodies
     of lovers
The lie of original sin

Always having for her the strongest love
Is not difficult
But everything is doubtful for the hearts of fire, the hearts of
     the faithful

Always having the strongest love
There are no unintentional betrayals
The flesh never lies
And the body of the most vicious remains pure

Pure like the great love for her
In my heart alone it flows without constraint
No mind ever touches my image of her
The only beloved in the heart of the lover.

No mind ever touches the great love for her
It is for its purity that one admires the diamond
No mud stains the diamond nor her heart
The only beloved in the heart of the lover

The sincerest lover is capable of the strongest love
Neither chaste nor ascetic nor puritanical
And if he tries the bodies of others more beautiful
It is because he knows well the most beautiful is that of his love

Le plus sincère amant est un débauché
Sa bouche a connu et éprouve tous les baisers
Se livrerait-il à tous les vices
Il n'en vaudrait que mieux

Car le plus sincère amant s'il n'est pas aimé par celle qu'il aime
Peu lui importe, il l'aimera
Éternellement désirera d'être aimé
Et d'aimer sans espoir deviendra pur comme un diamant.

Tout son corps ne sera qu'une proie décevante
Pour les fausses amantes et pour les faux amours
Et sans pitié l'amant le véritable sacrifiera tout pour celle
  qu'il aime

Qu'importe s'il a toujours le plus grand amour pour elle
Au jour de la rencontre désirée
Il sera plus pur que l'aube et le feu
Et prêt pour l'extase

Toujours avoir le plus grand amour pour elle
Il n'y a pas de trahison corporelle
Et que ton cœur batte toujours pour elle
Que tes yeux se ferment sur son unique image.

Être aimé par elle
Nul bonheur nulle félicité
Désir pas même
Mais volonté ou plutôt destin

{The sincerest lover is debauched
His mouth has felt and sampled every kiss
If he were to indulge in every vice
So much the better}

For the most sincere lover if he isn't loved by the one he loves
It's not important, he will love
Eternally desiring to be loved
And from loving without hope will become pure like a diamond.

All his body will be deceptive prey
For the false mistresses and untrue lovers
And without pity
The true lover will sacrifice all for the one he loves

What does it matter if he always feels this strong love for her
To the day they'll finally meet
He will be more pure than the dawn and the fire
And ready for the ecstasy

Always having the strongest love for her
He does not feel a bodily betrayal
And that your heart beats always for her
That your eyes close on her unique image.

To be loved by her
Neither happiness nor bliss
Desire not for the self
But for will or even destiny

Être aimé par elle
Non pas une nuit de toutes les nuits
Mais à jamais pour l'éternel présent
Sans paysage et sans lumières

Être aimé par elle
Écrit dans les signes du temps
Malgré tout contre antan et futur
A jamais

Mais pour être aimé par elle
Faut-il perdre jusqu'à l'amour
La vie n'en parlons pas
L'amour l'amour non plus

Être aimé par elle
C'est inévitable
Pas de chants pas de cris
Nul sentiment

Être aimé par elle
Marbre impassible Mers figées Ciels implacables
Mais attendre attendre longtemps attendre encore
Attendre? nié par l'éternité.

Mourir après elle
Est le rôle dévolu à l'amant
A lui seul le droit suprême
De graver un nom sur une pierre périssable

To be loved by her
Neither for one night or all nights
But to be forever in the eternal present
Without landscape and without lights

To be loved by her
Written in the sign of the times
Still against yesteryear and the future
To never

But to be loved by her
It is necessary to lose the love
The life we are not speaking of
The love the love no longer

To be loved by her
It is inevitable
Neither songs nor cries
No sentiment

To be loved by her
Untouched marble   Frozen rivers   Ruthless skies
But to wait to wait a long time & to still wait
To wait?   to stop at eternity.

To die after her
Is the role given to the lover
To him alone is given the supreme right
To engrave a name on the perishable stone

De graver un nom sur un arbre périssable
Et de s'éteindre pour jamais
S'éteindre lui après elle
Mais l'amour le plus grand amour
Brûlera comme une flamme éternelle.

Depuis de si longs mois, ma chère, que je t'aime
Pourquoi ne pas vouloir connaître mes travaux ?
Si mes jours sont soumis à de mornes systèmes
Mes nuits sont escortées par de nobles prévôts.

Dois-je veiller encore un bûcher renaissant,
Si vif que le Phénix ne pourrait y survivre,
Ou dois-je, naufragé, vers les vaisseaux passant
Effeuiller sans raison les pages de ce livre ?

Dois-je m'anéantir pour éteindre ma foi ?
L'univers de mon rêve exalte ton image
Mais les pays fameux que j'ai créés pour toi
Seront-ils traversés mieux que par ton mirage ?

S'il faut mourir au pied des idoles rivales,
Je suis prêt. Confessant ta cruelle grandeur
Je mourrai si tu veux pour n'être en tes annales
Que l'écho faiblissant d'une inutile ardeur.

Je donne tout pour toi, jusqu'au cœur des fantômes,
Soumis à mon fatal et délicieux tourment
Quitte pour disparaître en deux lignes d'un tome
Et sans être invoqué le soir par les amants.

To engrave a name on a perishable tree
And to never pass away
To pass away after her
But the strongest love
Burns like an eternal flame.

For so many long months, my dear, I've loved you
Why do you not want to know my work?
If my days are subject to dismal plans
My nights are accompanied by noble provosts.

Ought I to stay awake late reviving the pyre
So alone that the Phoenix would not be able to survive,
Or ought I, shipwrecked, towards the passing vessels
Toss without reason the pages of this book?

Shouldn't I annihilate myself in order to extinguish my faith?
The universe of my dream exalts your image
But will the famous country that I have created for you
Be traveled across better than by your mirage?

If it is necessary to die at the feet of rival idols
I am ready. Confessing your great cruelty
I will die if you wish in order not to be in your annals
Where the echo is weakened by useless ardor.

I give everything to you, down to the heart of the ghosts,
Submit it to my fatal and delicate torment
Leave in order to disappear in two lines of a book
Without having invoked the evening of lovers.

Je suis las de combattre un sort qui se dérobe,
Las de tenter l'oubli, las de me souvenir
Du moindre des parfums émanant de ta robe,
Las de te détester et las de te bénir.

Je valais mieux que ça mais tu l'as méconnu.
Un jour d'entre les jours de soleil sur les roches
Souviens-toi de l'amant dont le cœur était nu
Et qui sut te servir sans peur et sans reproche.

Attends-tu que j'aborde à de lointains rivages
Pour dire en regardant tes genoux désertés :
« Qui donc s'en est allé, j'ignore son visage
« Mais pourquoi s'en va-t-il seul vers sa liberté ?

« Il faut le retrouver, serviteur infidèle,
« L'enchaîner à mon bagne après l'avoir châtié
« Et qu'il me serve encore avec un cœur modèle
« Sans même pour sa peine éprouver ma pitié.

« Car je suis impérieuse et veux qu'on m'obéisse,
« Nul ne doit me quitter sans être congédié
« Tant pis pour celui-là qui rentre à mon service
« Si son orgueil hautain ne l'a pas répudié.

« Je connais pour les cœurs des prisons fantasques :
« Que l'amant fugitif y retourne au plus tôt
« Car il me faut ce soir de nombreux domestiques
« Pour cirer mes souliers et m'offrir le manteau. »

I am tired of fighting the destiny which conceals me
Tired of trying to forget, tired of remembering
The slightest perfume which rises from your dress,
Tired of hating you and blessing you.

I was better than that but you misunderstood me.
One day among the sunny days on the rocks
Do you remember the love whose heart was hurt
And who knew to serve you without fear and without reproval?

Do you expect me to reach the far-off shores
In order to speak regarding your bare knees:
"Whoever has gone away, I ignore his face
But why does he go alone towards his liberty?

It is necessary to rediscover him, unfaithful servant,
To chastise him then throw him into prison
So that he will serve me again with a model heart
Without even feeling pity for his pain.

For I am domineering and want him to obey me,
And never leave me without being dismissed.
So much worse for the one who re-enters my service
If his lofty pride is not renounced.

I knew the hearts of fantastic prisons:
The fugitive lover will return there at the earliest
For I need this evening a number of servants
To polish my shoes and help me with my coat."

A quoi bon? L'évadé connaît bien sa prison.
Sans doute a-t-il choisi de trop précieux otages
Pour vouloir à nouveau te payer sa rançon ;
Les trésors d'un cœur pur ne souffrent pas partage.

Évade-toi de l'eau, des prisons, des potences,
Adieu, je partirai comme on meurt un matin.
Ce ne sont pas les lieues qui feront la distance
Mais ces mots : Je l'aimais! murmurés au lointain.

Adorable signe inscrit dans les eaux mortes
Profondeurs boueuses
Ô poissons qui rôdez autour des algues
Où est la source que j'entends couler depuis si longtemps et
    que je n'ai jamais rencontrée
Qui ferme sans cesse des portes lourdes et sonores?
Eaux mortes Source invisible
Criminel attends-moi au détour du sentier parmi les grandes
    ciguës.
Pareilles aux nuages les soirées sans raison naissent et meurent
    avec ce tatouage au-dessus du sein gauche : Demain
L'eau s'écoule lentement par une fêlure de la bouteille où les
    plus fameux astrologues viennent boire l'élixir de vie
Tandis que l'homme aux yeux clos ne sait que répéter :
    « Une cigogne de perdue deux de retrouvées »
Et que les ciguës se fanent dans l'ombre du rendez-vous
Et que demain ponctuel mais masqué en costume de
    prud'homme ouvre un grand parapluie rouge au milieu de
    la prairie où sèche le linge des fermières de l'aube.

To what good? The fugitive knows the prison well.
Without doubt he has chosen too many precious hostages
In order to pay you his ransom:
The treasures of a pure heart do not allow sharing.

Escape from the water, the prisons, the gallows,
Goodbye, as one who bruises the morning I depart.
There are no places which have the distance
Of the words: I loved you! murmured from far away.

Divine sign inscribed in the stagnant waters
Muddy bottoms
O fish who prowl around the algae
Where is the spring which I heard running for such a long time
    and which I have never encountered
Who closes without stopping the heavy and sonorous doors?
Stagnant waters Invisible source
A criminal waits for me at the turn of the path among the giant
    hemlock plants.
Like the clouds evening parties are born without reason and
    die with this tattoo on top of the left breast: Tomorrow
The water flows slowly from a crack in the bottle where the
    most famous astrologers come to drink the elixir of life
While the man with his eyes closed only repeats:
    "For every stork lost two are found"
And the hemlock fades in the shadow of our meeting
And tomorrow punctual but masked in the costume of a man
    of experience a great red umbrella opens in the middle of
    the prairie where the linen of the farmer's wife dries from
    a paddle.

Blêmes effigies fantômes de marbre dressés dans les palais
    nocturnes
Une lame de parquet craque
Une épée tombe toute seule et se fiche dans le sol
Et je marche sans arrêt à travers une succession
De grandes salles vides dont les parquets cirés ont le reflet
    de l'eau.
Il y a des mains dans cette nuit de marais
Une main blanche et qui est comme un personnage vivant
Et qui est la main sur laquelle je voudrais poser mes lèvres
    et où je n'ose pas les poser.

Il y a les mains terribles
Main noircie d'encre de l'écolier triste
Main rouge sur le mur de la chambre du crime
Main pâle de la morte
Mains qui tiennent un couteau ou un revolver
Mains ouvertes
Mains fermées
Mains abjectes qui tiennent un porte-plume
Ô ma main toi aussi toi aussi
Ma main avec tes lignes et pourtant c'est ainsi
Pourquoi maculer tes lignes mystérieuses
Pourquoi? plutôt les menottes plutôt te mutiler plutôt plutôt
Écris écris car c'est une lettre que tu écris a elle et ce moyen
    impur est un moyen de la toucher
Mains qui se tendent mains qui s'offrent
Y a-t-il une main sincère parmi elles
Ah je n'ose plus serrer les mains
Mains menteuses mains lâches mains que je hais

Hideous ghosts phantoms of marble rise in the nocturnal palace
A cracked floorboard
A sword falling all alone and pointing towards the sun
And I walk without stopping through a succession
Of large empty rooms whose waxed floors have the reflection
    of water.
There are some hands on this foggy night
A white hand that is like a living person
And that is the hand on which I would like to place my lips
    & where I dare not place them.

There are terrible hands
Hand black from the ink of a sad schoolboy
Hand red on the wall of the room of crime
Hand pale as death
Hands which hold a knife or a revolver
Hands opened
Hands closed
Wretched hands grasping a pen holder
O my hand you too you too
My hand with your lines and yet if it is so
Why do you stain your mysterious lines
Why? more handcuffs more mutilation more more
Write write for it is a letter that you write to her & this impure
    way is a way of touching her
Hands that stretch hands that soften
Is there a sincere hand among them
Ah I no longer dare to shake hands
Lying hands loose hands hands that I mangle

Mains qui avouent et qui tremblent quand je regarde les yeux
Y a-t-il encore une main que je puisse serrer avec confiance
Mains sur la bouche de l'amour
Mains sur le cœur sans amour
Mains au feu de l'amour
Mains à couper du faux amour
Mains basses sur l'amour
Mains mortes à l'amour
Mains forcées pour l'amour
Mains levées sur l'amour
Mains tenues sur l'amour
Mains hautes sur l'amour
Mains tendues vers l'amour
Mains d'œuvre d'amour
Mains heureuses d'amour
Mains à la pâte hors l'amour horribles mains
Mains liées par l'amour éternellement
Mains lavées par l'amour par des flots implacables
Mains à la main c'est l'amour qui rôde
Mains pleines c'est encore l'amour
Mains armées c'est le véritable amour
Mains de maître mains de l'amour
Main chaude d'amour
Main offerte à l'amour
Main de justice main d'amour
Main forte à l'amour!

Mains Mains toutes les mains
Un homme se noie une main sort des flots

Hands clasped in the prayer of one who trembles when I look
    him in the eye
Is there still a hand I am able to shake with confidence
Hands on the lover's mouth
Hands on the heart without love
Hands cut by false love
Hands founded on love
Hands closed to love
Hands dead to love
Hands straining for love
Hands rising for love
Hands held for love
Hands high on love
Hands tender towards love
Hands open with love
Hands happy from love
Horrible hands stained for love only
Hands tied by eternal love
Hands washed by loves' relentless waves
Hand to hand it is love which prowls
Hands full again for love
Hands armed it is true love
Hands of the master hands of the lover
Hands warm from love
Hands open to love
Hand of justice hand of love
Hand strong from love!

Hands hands all the hands
A man grows black a hand knows some waves

Un homme s'en va une main s'agite
Une main se crispe un cœur souffre
Une main se ferme ô divine colère
Une main encore une main
Une main sur mon épaule
Qui est-ce?
Est-ce toi enfin?
Il fait trop sombre! quelles ténèbres!
Je ne sais plus à qui sont les mains
Ce qu'elles veulent
Ce qu'elles disent
Les mains sont trompeuses
Je me souviens encore de mains blanches dans l'obscurité
    étendues sur une table dans l'attente
Je me souviens de mains dont l'étreinte m'était chère
Et je ne sais plus
Il y a trop de traîtres trop de menteurs
Ah même ma main qui écrit
Un couteau! une arme! un outil!
Tout sauf écrire!
Du sang du sang!

Patience! ce jour se lèvera.

Églantines flétries parmi les herbiers
Ô feuilles jaunes
Tout craque dans cette chambre
Comme dans l'allée nocturne les herbes sous le pied.
De grandes ailes invisibles immobilisent mes bras et le
    retentissement d'une mer lointaine parvient jusqu'à moi.

A man goes away a hand is shaking
A hand clenches a heart suffers
A hand closes O divine passion
A hand & again a hand
A hand on my shoulder
Who is it?
Is it you finally?
It is too overcast! What shadows!
I no longer know to whom are these hands
These she wants
These she says
The hands are misleading
I can still remember some white hands in the darkness
    outspread on the table in expectation
I can remember hands whose embrace was dear to me
And I don't know anything
There are too many traitors too many liars
Ah the very hand which writes
A knife!   an arm!   a tool!
All except writing!
In blood in blood!

Patience!   the day will come.

Wild dog rose withers among grass sheds
O yellow leaves
All crackle in this room
Like grass snapping underfoot in a dark alley.
Great invisible wings immobilize my arms and the echoing
    of a distant sea reaches me.

Le lit roule jusqu'à l'aube sa bordure d'écume et l'aube ne
    paraît pas
Ne paraîtra jamais.
Verre pilé, boiseries pourries, rêves interminables, fleurs flétries,
Une main se pose à travers les ténèbres toute blanche sur
    mon front,
Et j'écouterai jusqu'au jour improbable
Voler en se heurtant aux murailles et aux meubles l'oiseau
    de paradis, l'oiseau que j'ai enfermé par mégarde
Rien qu'en fermant les yeux.

Jamais l'aube à grands cris bleuissant les lavoirs,
L'aube, savon trempé dans l'eau des fleuves noirs,
L'aube ne moussera sur cette nuit livide
Ni sur nos doigts tremblants ni sur nos verres vides.
C'est la nuit sans frontière et fille des sapins
Qui fait grincer au port la chaîne des grappins
Nuit des nuits sans amour étrangleuse du rêve
Nuit de sang nuit de feu nuit de guerre sans trêve
Nuit de chemin perdu parmi les escaliers
Et de pieds retombant trop lourds sur les paliers
Nuit de luxure nuit de chute dans l'abîme
Nuit de chaînes sonnant dans la salle du crime
Nuit de fantômes nus se glissant dans les lits
Nuit de réveil quand les dormeurs sont affaiblis.
Sentant rouler du sang sur leur maigre poitrine
Et monter à leurs dents la bave de l'angine
Ils caressent dans l'ombre un vampire velu
Et ne distinguent pas si le monstre goulu

The light rolls until the edge of dawn froths and dawn does
    not appear
Nothing appears.
Ground glass, decaying woodwork, endless dreams, withering
    flowers
A totally white hand rises through the shadows of my forehead
And I will listen to the improbable day
To fly and knock myself against the walls and the furniture,
    a bird of paradise, a bird which I have inadvertently
    locked away
Only closing my eyes.

If ever dawn to great cries turns the bathing houses blue
The dawn, soap soaked in the water of black rivers,
Dawn will not sparkle on this gray night
Nor on the trembling fingers nor on the empty glasses.
It is the night without frontier and fir trees
Who grinds at the chain of the anchor at the port
Night of nights without love strangled from the dream
Night of blood night of fire night of war without truce
Night of a lost path among the stairs
And of the feet falling too heavily onto the landing
Night of luxury night of the fall into the abyss
Night of the chains ringing in the room of the criminals
Night of naked ghosts gliding in the beds
Night of waking when the sleepers are weak.
To feel the blood pass into their thin chests
And to shower their teeth with the spittle of the heart
In the shadow they caress a hairy vampire
And are unable to distinguish of the greedy monster

N'est pas leur cœur battant sous leurs côtes souillées.
Nuit d'échos indistincts et de braises mouillées
Nuit d'incendies étincelant sur les miroirs
Nuit d'aveugle cherchant des sous dans les tiroirs
Nuit des nuits sans amour, où les draps se dérobent,
Où sur les boulevards sifflent les policiers
Ô nuit! cruelle nuit où frissonnent des robes
Où chuchotent des voix au chevet des malades,
Nuit dose pour jamais par des verrous d'acier
Nuit ô nuit solitaire et sans astre et sans rade!

Dans tes yeux, dans ton cœur et dans le ciel aussi
Vois s'étoiler soudain l'univers imprécis,
La fissure grandir étroite et lumineuse
Comme si quelque fauve aux griffes paresseuses
Avait étreint la nuit et l'avait déchirée
(Mais la lueur sera pâle et lente la marée)
Des nervures courir dans le cristal fragile
Des fêlures mimer des couleuvres agiles
Qui rouleraient et se noueraient dans la lueur
Pâle d'une aube étrange. Ainsi lorsque le joueur
Fatigué de tourner les cartes symboliques
Voit le matin cruel éclairer les portiques
Maintes pensées et maints désirs presque oubliés
Maints éventails flétris tombent sur les paliers.

Tais-toi, pose la plume et ferme les oreilles
Aux pas lents et pesants qui montent l'escalier.
La nuit déjà pâlit mais cette aube est pareille
A des papillons morts au pied des chandeliers.

Is not their own heart thrashing in their soiled sides.
Night of indistinct echoes and wet charcoal
Night of fires sparkling in the mirrors
Night of the blind looking for some sous in the drawers
Night of nights without love, where the bedsheets slip away,
Where the police whistle on the boulevards
O night!   cruel night where the rustling of the robes
Where the whispering of the voices at the bedside of the sick,
Night closed forever by a steel bolt
Night O lonely night without star or anchor!

In your eyes, in your heart and in the sky also
I see suddenly the stars of the impressive universe,
The crack growing narrow and luminous
As if some wild animal with sluggish claws
Had embraced the night and mangled it
(But the gleam will be pale and the tide slow)
From nerves running in the fragile crystal
Cracks miming the agile grass snakes
Who run and become one with the light
Pale from a strange dawn. Thus when
The tired player turns the symbolic cards
To see the cruel morning light from the porches
Many a thought and many a desire almost forgotten
Many a withered fan falls on the landings.

Be quiet, lay down your pen and close your eyes
To the slow and heavy steps which mount the stairs.
The night has already grown pale but this dawn is similar
To some dead butterflies at the foot of the candlesticks.

Une tempête de fantômes sacrifie
Tes yeux qui les défient aux larmes du désir.
Quant au ciel, plus fané qu'une photographie
Usée par les regards, il n'est qu'un long loisir.

Appelle la sirène et l'étoile à grands cris
Si tu ne peux dormir bouche close et mains jointes
Ainsi qu'un chevalier de pierre qui sourit
A voir le ciel sans dieux et les enfers sans plainte.

Ô Révolte!

A storm of ghosts sacrificed
Your eyes which challenge them to the tears of desire.
As for the sky, more faded than a photograph
Worn away by looking at it, like a long expanse of leisure.

With great cries call the siren and the star
If you are unable to sleep close your mouth and join hands
Like a knight of stone who smiles
To see no god in the sky and hell without suffering.

Revolt!

Desnos and Warsh: Dreaming as One

IN 1971, HOLED UP IN TORONTO, I received an envelope from my Buffalo draft lawyer containing a terse telegram from Attorney General John Mitchell: "Rosenberg charges dropped," and soon I was back in NYC. I edited issues 9–12 of my formerly Toronto-based poetry magazine, *The Ant's Forefoot*, on St. Mark's Place. It was 1973, nearly a half-century after Robert Desnos wrote *Night of Loveless Nights*, and a half-century ago from today, that I gave over an issue of my mag to Lewis Warsh's translation, while his Angel Hair Books printed my first translations of the psalms.

As it happened: Lewis came by with the mimeograph stencils for my *Some Psalms and* casually showed me his Desnos for *The Ant's Forefoot*. (He was its most regular contributor, having been in every issue over six years.) It appeared he had completed the Desnos just that week, perhaps even in a single night, which was hardly démodé in the speedy early '70s when Warsh took over the poem—yet dawn was different, it was time to go out for a Pepsi at Gem Spa à la the great Ted Berrigan. Still, we can't quite imagine Desnos or Warsh doing that; their sense of lost love wasn't so much a defying of depression as post-tragic, almost heroic in their poem's struggle to recast love as poetry, ultimately wedded to revival, to dawn. It was a refashioned epithalamium. What's more, Warsh's text preserved a whiff of what earlier surrealists like Desnos called "automatic" writing, and which Desnos in particular had experimented with, calling it "sleep-writing."

I read it through as we shared a joint, amazed at how long it was for a single entry in the mag's next issue. Did Lewis expect me to excerpt from it? I decided on the spot I didn't want to contemplate that; it had to be its own issue, a book. So, in 1973, *Night of Loveless Nights* became the first book by Desnos to be translated and published in English.

The Warsh/Desnos book, Issue 10 of *The Ant's Forefoot*, was printed at Brooklyn's CCLM grant-supported Print Center. Both Angel Hair Books and *The Ant's Forefoot* had by that time devolved from luxe papers and printings to mimeographed editions, and, in the case of the Desnos, to faux offset printing (Linotype printing onto paper plates) and saddle-stitched binding. Our reduction to stark realism was not only a commitment to survival, budget-wise, but a minimalist aesthetic. Every graphic aspect of my edition of *Night* was deluxe minimalism: the leftover paper stock I scrounged was complemented by exquisite late-night typesetting and layout on non-uniform page size, including a slight bleeding/aging process to the dreamy archival photos Lewis added for illustration. It's impossible to reproduce; the materials of that impoverished graphic arts scene are long gone.

The poem was originally published in French in 1930, a month before the poems' inspiration—the Belgian-French chanteuse Yvonne George—died an early death. In 1926, when Desnos composed his *Night*, he would have seen Greta Garbo in the silent, *Torrent*. "If only to steal a perfect hour, it will never come again," she says in intertitles. Facing his lost love of Yvonne, Desnos's poem is a companion to Garbo's "perfect hour." The formal French alexandrines that trellis the poem echo Yvonne's lyrics, yet his voice, like hers, soars apart.

My prior sense of Desnos was informed by John Ashbery's intro to the *Collected Poems* of Frank O'Hara, in '71. John felt that Frank had founded a new postwar tradition in American poetry: to speak not so much *in* a poem as *with* it, even a sort of conversing in which the poem could speak for itself, with something especially to say about poetry.

The French context of Desnos's *Night* is hyper-irony, as well as opium-irony, something deeper in its use of poetic tradition than the general English-language pot-irony of the '70s. That is why I think Desnos wasn't translated by poets in that day, who otherwise made much of Apollinaire and company. The damn alexandrines were something only Rimbaud could have appreciated (were he still alive). Yet that form is but a flamenco tambourine beneath Desnos' visionary comédie-tragique. And that is why Lewis, who had translated little else and whose French was slow, felt he could do it as he did, as if taking dictation for a poem of his own. Most translators wouldn't be up to it poetically. Alice Notley was, but somewhat later, in her free translations within *Désamère* (O Books, 1995).

Less ambitious than Lewis when he translated that small book of an epic poem, I myself had translated some short ones by Desnos:

Dialogue

—Nothing interests me

—Laughs, lovingly, Therese

Actually, of course, Desnos is quite interested in Therese, but she fails to take him seriously. Which one is alive? In this tiny poem, Therese resurrects him from the dead of "nothing," so that Desnos can lose her again: she is enlivened only by the poem. Or: Therese is in dialogue with herself, doubly distant in her self-love. What it can't be is an homage; it'd be a burlesque of a coquette. So, is it comedy or tragedy? Rather, it's a blues. With these six words, the trimeter is stretched from nothing (as it were) in the first line to a double caesura in the second.

With this little piece, among others, Desnos had brought American blues to Paris, to underscore the jazz age. Here, it's an advance on the strength of imagism in Pound's "The apparition of these faces in the crowd: / Petals on a wet, black bough." What Pound called "an intellectual and emotional complex in an instant of time" has become, within almost the same period and place (both poems were written in Paris), more of an intellectual and emotional *drama* in Desnos's instant of time.

Night of Loveless Nights works hundreds of lines to the same effect. It invokes every mode from epic to lyric, yet it's none of them, nor is it Apollinaire's early jazz. It's a solo theater of the blues, an orchestration of despair raised to the level of a post-devil-may-care postwar goodbye to romantic, unrequited love. It may have seemed complementary to Ravel's *Boléro* (written as a ballet first performed at the Paris Opera in 1928) yet it can't be danced. Desnos is glued to his seat, his girl off with another man. Actually, *the* man, in drug parlance. (That's a biographical note; she isn't named in the poem.) Perhaps it's the first blues performed without an audience, and this is what Lewis Warsh's translation confirms like no other.

* * *

IN 1944, THE YEAR LEWIS WARSH was born, Robert Desnos was arrested in Paris by the Gestapo and eventually arrived to Auschwitz, via Drancy. Had Desnos lived beyond his demise in the Holocaust's death camps—age 44, tracked down in Paris as both Jew and *resistant*—after the war, he would probably have put aside the blues or surrealism (the movement within which he'd been a storied dreamer). Although it cheapens the word surreal to apply it to death camps, the Auschwitz-surviving French-language novelist Piotr Rawicz, in *Blood from the Sky* (Gallimard, 1961) did push surrealism into a realistic dark alley, from where it comes out bloodied but still breathing. I take Rawicz's novel (twice translated into English) as a marker for how Desnos might have proceeded, had he survived. In Anthony Rudolf's chapter entitled "The Companion of a Dream" (in *Engraved in Flesh*, Menard Press, 1996, 2007) this excerpt from Rawicz on his character:

> A quarter of a century ago, in a death cell where the emissaries of this city shut you up, you swallowed a quantity of cyanide. And you survived. That, at least, is what is claimed. And then, other dreams are reborn in a garret in an old quarter of Paris between a man and a woman who do not succeed in loving each other, for they are but a single non-being.

That "single non-being" reminds me of Lewis's early book-title, *Dreaming as One* (Corinth, 1971). Nevertheless, if Blues derived from surviving slavery, *Blood from the Sky* derives from surviving death-slavery in Auschwitz. In Lawrence Langer's intro to Peter Wiles's translation of the novel (Harcourt, 1964; Yale, 2003; updated by Rudolf in 2009 for Elliot & Thompson) Langer wrote: "Its sense of artistic urgency is driven less by moral fervor than by the compulsion to witness."

Did Warsh have such an angle on Desnos in mind, even as in his own work he uniquely domesticated becoming a witness? When we might think the quotidian history on the page is ready to be framed, contextualized, it is only an as if—for any context turns into a story: "no more stories" (*Piece of Cake*, Station Hill, 2020). (We could say that Lewis's collaboration with Bernadette Mayer on *Piece of Cake* was the domesticated Gertrude Stein, evoking her collaboration with Alice B. Toklas on the autobiography.) Instead, we see the mind at its natural work—like a postwar bebop saxophone suppressing the melody. This is art resolved into witness—post-Objectivist but still rendered a necessity by a horrendous century. Warsh's novels forced our attention from narrative to the artless sentences. "Brightlingsea sounds good" he wrote to me while I briefly lived there. It was impossible for him to write the simplest thing sans the complexity of timing or sound. And speaking of bebop, Lewis in early 2020, still expecting another remission from his cancer, wrote to me that behind the New York hospital room's screen, the man alternately snoring and humming riffs in the next bed, two decades his senior, was legendary saxophonist Lee Konitz.

We were twenty-somethings when we took the French avant-garde poets in primarily the 1920s, from Max Jacob to Pierre Reverdy, as our forefathers of deadpan, no less than Louis Armstrong: it was the decade in which American jazz riveted Paris. Stein, Breton—they were a bit too programatic for our sensibilities, though Stein was in our blood and manifested later. But Robert Desnos (1900–1945) was in-between; he seemed to push through surrealism and come out on the other side as a literal dreamer, in search of reality and lost love. Desnos's dreamer was parallel to a soul, disembodied—not the disordered mind's "we must change life" of Rimbaud. Desnos was more grounded by loss. In *A New Theory for American Poetry* (Harvard, 2004), Angus Fletcher compared Ashbery to Desnos: "A French tonality touches his new surrealist style of sensibility, which to my ear recalls the rhythms of a poet like Robert Desnos." We were reading Ashbery back in '73, when Lewis translated Desnos, but we were less close to the "rhythms" and more to what Fletcher describes as "a certain tenderness" in Ashbery.

Lewis finds the root note in *Night of Loveless Nights* at the tender bottom of its surrealist chords: "lover / whose pain never dies." I think we first heard it in our own neighborhood from Ted Berrigan, who might translate "dream" for "pain." But Ted's sleepless night was no dream; in fact, it was a dismantling of dreams, down to the soul walking its East Village sidewalks, just happy to have a bodily home. Joseph Joubert was ironic in his 1796 notebook—"I will build a temple for the worship of dreams," in Paul Auster's translation—a dream in itself. Desnos's poem might be a dream temple in this sense: he is passionately searching for a way out, to ultimately arrive at "Many a withered fan falls on the landings./ Be quiet, lay down your pen and close your eyes." That line in the poem's penultimate stanza foretells the last stanza's "If you are unable to sleep"... you might become "Like a knight of stone... Revolt!" Desnos's revolt is a most tender revolution against written dreaTms, for it's daylight now, and you are alive, whether asleep or awake.

* * *

THERE ARE LIVELY AND MORE COMPLETE collections of Desnos in English by Mary Ann Caws and Timothy Adès, but Lewis Warsh's *Night of Loveless Nights* is unique, a sublime translation experiment as is rarely brought off. While Warsh's New York poet-colleagues subsequently produced exquisite versions of Blaise Cendrars (Ron Padgett) and Arthur Rimbaud (John Ashbery), Warsh's Desnos lets the language speak for itself, just as it did when it became restless and indefatigable in Desnos's hands. The almost-alive text is willful and wildly subdued, what we used to call deadpan (today it's almost a lost art).

"Can we mount an authentic performance as Shakespeare would have seen it? No. Authenticity in the performing arts is ultimately impossible." So writes Peter Hall in *Shakespeare's Advice to the Players* (TCG, 2003). Saying the same for literary translation seems a commonplace—except the word "performing" reminds us that, in the sense a written poem is a performance on the page, a poem in translation may come alive when the new performance echoes the original in quality. Beyond Pound's *Cantos* ("Nothing matters but the quality / of the affection— / in the end—that has carved the trace in the mind") what matters is that the translator makes his/their struggle to echo—i.e. *befriend*—the original, palpable.

Adès, among his extensive and important Desnos translations (Arc, 2017), ardently engages the *text* of Desnos's poem. If you're a structuralist you'll sympathize with its almost hysterical pitch of textual drama. But is Desnos an opera singer? Lewis Warsh doesn't think so. He is in rapport with the poet himself and his plumbing the depth of his love—or more accurately, his love for the lost. What kind of love is that? It's between the poem's muse and the life story behind it: Which will win, the poem or the life? Desnos apparently moved on; now it becomes Warsh's agon.

Back in '73, Lewis and I commiserated on recent broken relationships. He maintained friendship with ex-wife and Angel Hair collaborator Anne Waldman, as he seemed to do with everyone in his life, and as Desnos had tried to with Yvonne. Adès writes: "The night-club singer Yvonne George was dying of drink and drugs. [Desnos] worked through this difficult period with a series of big poems... ending with an epic, *The Night of Loveless Nights.*" For Lewis, Yvonne and Anne dissolve into a bodiless love of language, a tenderness for it, a mother tongue, the child's drive to hear the sense of it, but always beyond him, and as in Warsh's later work, often turning into collage.

Of Desnos, Adès wrote that he "experimented with montage and collage to generate associative leaps across kinds of language and registers of meaning." However, in his own translation, Adès's meter and rhyme contrast with Warsh's dedication to a disembodied language speaking as if on its own:

> Adès:
> "Women with white panties underneath a skirt"
>
> Warsh:
> "Who, under their skirts, wear a pair of white pants"

In the French, it is *pantalon*—literally pants, rather than *culotte*, suggesting panties. This may seem minor, but it's one of many instances where Warsh's translation reveals its devotion to the language having its own sense: "pants" is generic but also surprising in this female context because it reminds us *language by itself* is blind, and thereby gender blind. You could imagine the poet's brain was down there on the page, not thinking or ruminating but intensely curious about its disembodied state shaped by inexact words—curious as well to be looking back at its body behind the typewriter. Except Desnos was looking at himself bereft at the keyboard, love lost, the passion still driving onward of itself. I tried to graphically translate that thought to the cover image (reproduced in this volume), which depicts the ghost of Desnos adding disembodied hands to the typewriter.

In 2020, while he still somewhat hoped for a remission, Lewis suggested he might do a Zoom poetry workshop entitled "How to Continue." He was referring to the pandemic, but I hear it now as the lifelong Warshian drive morphing into poetic afterlife. Later that year, his last on earth, Lewis told me he'd reread his 47-year-old translation, and was startled by its tonic relevance to late life.

Actually, Lewis had always stalked the literal history, just as his translation tries to drag Desnos into common sense while the poem gets away from both of them. Although the text of the poem sounds heroically bigger than himself, the wounded poet behind it is crucial to Warsh. Each of them, Desnos and Warsh, was a connoisseur of the labor of writing; that is, for Warsh especially, the double work of writing as reading; and what Lewis was reading in his own or in Desnos's lines was the "*almost* surreal." In the essay, "Richard Wright's Blues," Ralph Ellison writes: "Like a blues sung by such an artist as Bessie Smith, [Wright's] lyrical prose evokes the paradoxical, almost surreal image of a black boy singing lustily as he probes his own grievous wound." Lewis as Bessie? No, it's the "*almost* surreal" that Warsh takes from *Night of Loveless*

Nights, in his devotion to the language itself speaking. Lewis's *Night* wants a Desnos that loses himself, however momentarily, in the language, letting it take over It wants what the "mecha" David in Kubrick/Spielberg's, *A I.*, is programmed to want—"to feel love." It wants to be the living Desnos and, momentarily, it succeeds, as does the robot in the film—but only for a day (or a *night*), alive to feeling love's loss.

* * *

LEWIS HAD WRITTEN MORE THAN ONCE on the legendary Canadian poet, bpNichol (1944–1988), as preeminent explorer of consciousness—from a review in *Poetry* magazine back in '67 to "The Music of Pure Thought" (*Open Letter*, 2009, accessible online at akabpnichol.net). "The real wandering, in the 1960s, was happening in real time," he wrote in '09. "Even yesterday is a distant memory, as far back as any past you might conjure up." Typically, Warsh refers to the actual poet, Barrie Phillip, behind the narrating bp, as does his close colleague, Alice Notley, when she writes (in the same issue) of "the speaking voice that the poet puts within and between the words: it's almost everything."

In that same journal, I'd written of "lost love" as I would have of Desnos and Warsh in '73:

> Nichol steps out of his poetic world to continually critique or reject it. But it's the stepping outside that is most unique, for it's only possible because Nichol created a "writer" in bp who is strong enough to do so... one with a psyche and unconscious, trapped in the human, for whom a return to unconditional love is

> requited in the mothering of language—at the expense of a real-world unrequited love, or lost love. [...] Thus is established in the early books of his *The Martyrology* the theme of a lifelong journey to an inevitable death—a journey of love in the remembrance of loss, and hatred of the false turns and false journeys that loss makes inevitable.

For Desnos and Warsh, that hatred is a form of grandiosity which language itself makes inevitable. They undercut it in *Night of Loveless Nights* by allowing it to exhaust itself in an anti-grand opera encompassing all the socialized manners of civilization—shedding them, as it were, by tossing them off extempore: "The air of the chase is extinguished"; "the contemptible ink at the bottom of an inkwell"; "the seductive necks of the beautiful, miserable women"; "the crystal heart"; "the beautiful mouth with the meat-eating teeth."

Desnos and Warsh journey out of hell with the saving methods of poetry. In French, Desnos explodes traditional meter and rhyme; in English, Warsh subverts conventional free verse. As Warsh describes it via Nichol, "You get the feeling of a person in dire need using everything in poetry at his disposal. It's like being in the middle of a blizzard, with a light at the end."

—*David Rosenberg, Miami, 2022*

Editor's Note

Robert Desnos's poem, originally titled in English as "The Night of Loveless Nights," first saw print in a private-press edition of 156 copies, with three illustrations by his friend, the artist George Malkine, published in Antwerp in 1930.

The present volume is a fiftieth-anniversary republication of Lewis Warsh's English translation, *Night of Loveless Nights*, first published in 1973 as issue #10 of *The Ant's Forefoot*, a little magazine edited by poet and translator David Rosenberg, in a saddle-stitched edition of 300 copies.

In its 1973 edition, Warsh's translation stood alone, without the French text *en face*. Our edition provides the French poem on the verso pages and adjusts the layout of Warsh's translation to cohere, in most respects, to the manner in which the poem appears in Desnos's *Domaine public* (Gallimard, 1953), adding drop caps in the style of the poem's 1930 edition. We have also restored a missing stanza on page 35, marked with braces, and generously translated by Mark Polizzotti for this edition. Otherwise, besides correcting a few minor typographic errors and editorial oversights, not being able to consult with its author, we have elected to preserve the translation's idiosyncrasies.

Winter Editions extends heartfelt thanks to the family of Lewis Warsh (Katt Lissard; Marie, Sophia, and Max Warsh) for their assistance.

French poet ROBERT DESNOS (1900–1945) was introduced to Paris Dada and André Breton through poet Benjamin Péret in 1919, and became an active member of the Surrealist group, known in particular for automatic writing. Desnos's circle included leaders of the literary vanguard Louis Aragon and Paul Éluard, as well as Pablo Picasso, Ernest Hemingway, Antonin Artaud, and John Dos Passos. In 1929, due to political differences, Breton removed Desnos from the Surrealists' ranks. He then joined Georges Bataille and Documents, signing an attack on Breton. Besides his numerous collections of poems, he wrote reviews of jazz and cinema, published three novels, worked in radio, and wrote the script for a film by Man Ray (*L'Étoile de mer*, 1928). During World War II, Desnos was an active member of the French Resistance. He was arrested by the Gestapo in late February 1944, deported to Auschwitz, then Buchenwald, and finally to Terezín where he died of typhoid.

LEWIS WARSH (1944–2020) was a writer, editor, publisher, educator, visual artist, and the author of over thirty volumes of poetry, fiction, and autobiography. He was co-founder, with Bernadette Mayer, of United Artists Magazine and Books; and with Anne Waldman, of Angel Hair Books and Magazine. He received grants from the National Endowment for the Arts, The American Poetry Review, and The Poetry Foundation. *Mimeo Mimeo* #7 (2012) was devoted to his poetry, fiction, collages, and to a bibliography of his work as a publisher and editor. A lifelong teacher, he was founding director of Long Island University's MFA Program in Creative Writing (2007–2013). His posthumous collection of poetry, *Elixir*, was published by Ugly Duckling Presse in 2022.

DAVID ROSENBERG's poetry, translation and nonfiction includes several books based upon his biblical translations: *Blues of the Sky* (Angel Hair), *The Book of J*, with Harold Bloom (Grove), *Lost Book of Paradise* (Hyperion), *Dreams of Being Eaten Alive* (Harmony), *A Literary Bible* (Counterpoint), and *A Life in a Poem* (Shearsman). He has received a Guggenheim Fellowship for nonfiction, a PEN prize for *A Poet's Bible*, and a Hopwood Special Award in poetry, among other distinctions.

Robert Desnos, *Night of Loveless Nights*
Translated from French by Lewis Warsh
Translation copyright © The Estate of Lewis Warsh, 2023

Originally published as *The Night of Loveless Nights* (Anvers, 1930). Translation originally published as issue #10 of *The Ant's Forefoot* (New York, 1973).

An earlier version of David Rosenberg's essay was published in print and online by *The Fortnightly Review* (UK).

ISBN 978-1-959708-03-2
LCCN: 2023930704

First Edition, 2023 — 1250 copies
Winter Editions, Brooklyn, New York
wintereditions.net

WE books are typeset in Heldane, a renaissance-inspired serif designed by Kris Sowersby for Klim Type Foundry, and Zirkon, a contemporary gothic designed by Tobias Rechsteiner for Grilli Type. The typesetting and covers are done by the editor following a series design created by Andrew Bourne. The cover image is based on one of George Malkine's illustrations for the 1930 edition of Robert Desnos's poem. Printed and bound in Lithuania by BALTO print.

 Winter Editions

Emily Simon, IN MANY WAYS

Garth Graeper, THE SKY BROKE MORE

Robert Desnos, NIGHT OF LOVELESS NIGHTS, tr. Lewis Warsh

Richard Hell, WHAT JUST HAPPENED

Marina Tëmkina & Miche Gérard, BOYS FIGHT
[co-published with Alder & Frankia]

Helio Oiticica, SECRET POETICS, tr. Rebecca Kosick
[co-published with Soberscove Press]

Monica McClure, THE GONE THING

Claire DeVoogd, PATTERN ABYSS

Ahmad Almallah, BORDER WISDOM

Heimrad Bäcker, ON DOCUMENTARY POETRY, tr. Patrick Greaney